TWO ROOMS

TWO ROOMS
POEMS
CONSTANCE MERRITT

LOUISIANA STATE UNIVERSITY PRESS
BATON ROUGE

Published by Louisiana State University Press
Copyright © 2009 by Constance Merritt
All rights reserved
Manufactured in the United States of America
LSU Press Paperback Original

DESIGNER: *Amanda McDonald Scallan*
TYPEFACE: *Whitman*, text; *Diotima and ATSackersGothic*, display

Library of Congress Cataloging-in-Publication Data

Merritt, Constance, 1966–
Two rooms : poems / Constance Merritt.
p. cm.
ISBN 978-0-8071-3519-8 (pbk. : alk. paper)
I. Title.
PS3563.E74536T86 2009
811'.54—dc22
                        2009013497

The paper in this book meets the guidelines for permanence and durability of the Committee on Production Guidelines for Book Longevity of the Council on Library Resources. ∞

Grateful acknowledgment is made to the editors of the following periodicals, in which the poems listed first appeared: "Assimilation Blues," "Only Human," "Too Late, My Mother Tells Me," *Callaloo* 23:1 (Winter 2000); "Rites of Passage," "A Song of Brothers: A Duet," *Crazyhorse* Number 59 (Winter 2000); "The Mind in the Act of Finding What Will Suffice," *Crossroads: Journal of the Poetry Society of America* No. 60 (Fall / Winter 2003); "Idolatry," "Insomnia," "Poor in All Else . . . ," "The Price of the Ticket," "Stove," "Underwater," *Descant* 32:2 (Summer 2001); "A Poem about Brahms Perhaps," "A Portrait," *The Nebraska Review* 28:2 (Summer 2000); "Counterpoint," *The New Yorker* (February 9, 2004) "Lying," *The New Yorker* (May 24, 2004); "Fool's Gold," *Poetry* CLXXXIV:4 (August 2004); "The Afterlife," "Before the Curtain," "For, as to Change," "From the Land of Shades," reprinted from *Prairie Schooner* 75:1 (Spring 2001), copyright University of Nebraska Press, 2001; "A Brief Essay On the Economy of Friendship," "Burdens," "Two Rooms," "Yeats in Love," reprinted from *Prairie Schooner* 76:4 (Winter 2002), copyright University of Nebraska Press, 2002; "apoliticalpoem," "The Mind in the Act of Finding What Will Suffice," reprinted from *Prairie Schooner* 78:2 (Summer 2004), copyright University of Nebraska Press, 2004; "Sedimentary Blues," "Triolet," reprinted from *Prairie Schooner* 79:2 (Summer 2005), copyright University of Nebraska Press, 2005; "Forecast," "The Pack," "Partial Rose," "Sieve," reprinted from *Prairie Schooner* 79:3 (Fall 2005), copyright University of Nebraska Press, 2005; "Deserted Beach," "Thorn Apple," reprinted from *Prairie Schooner* 81:1 (Spring 2007), copyright University of Nebraska Press, 2007; "Company," reprinted from *Prairie Schooner*, 81:4 (Winter 2007), copyright University of Nebraska Press, 2007; "Is Backing Away. Is Gone," "Moving-House Blues," *Quarterly West* (Autumn/Winter 2001); "Only Where There Is Floating," "Race Point," *Radcliffe Quarterly* 87:3 (Winter 2002). "Remembering Daisies" appears in *Ars Botanica*, a limited edition artist's book by Enid Mark (Wallingford, PA: Elm Press, 2004). The epigraph for "Before the Curtain" is an excerpt from "Transactions in a Field That's Overgrown" from *The Girl with Bees in Her Hair* by Eleanor Wilner. Used by permission of Copper Canyon Press.

Work on this collection was supported by a fellowship from the Radcliffe Institute for Advanced Study at Harvard University and by a Rona Jaffe Foundation Writers' Award. My thanks to these institutions.

for M.
where it rests

The only people for me are the mad ones, the ones who are mad to live, mad to talk, mad to be saved, desirous of everything at the same time, the ones who never yawn or say a commonplace thing, but burn, burn, burn, like fabulous yellow roman candles exploding like spiders across the stars and in the middle you see the blue centerlight pop and everybody goes "Awww!"
—JACK KEROUAC, *ON THE ROAD*

Making recoveries of young nakedness
And the lost vehemence the midnights hold.
—WALLACE STEVENS, "STARS AT TALLAPOOSA"

CONTENTS

Sedimentary Blues 1

I

Moving-House Blues 3
Two Rooms 4
A Poem about Brahms Perhaps 5
A Portrait 6
Triolet 7
Insomnia 8
Bo Peep Blues 9
Idolatry 10
Too Late, My Mother Tells Me 11
Saber-Tooth Blues 12

II

From the Land of Shades 13
Yeats in Love 14
A Brief Essay on the Economy
    of Friendship 16
Underwater 17
This Work of Holding 18
Rites of Passage 19
The Price of the Ticket 20
Burdens 21

III

The Afterlife 23
Alba 24
Improbable Prison's Sweet Mess 25
Poor in All Else . . . 26
Assimilation Blues 27
Only Human 28
Before the Curtain 29
The Pack 31
A Song of Brothers: A Duet 33
Stove 34
Is Backing Away. Is Gone 36
The Wheel 37

IV

As If I Had Invented It 39
From the Monk's Courtship 40
Only Where There Is Floating 43
Lying 44
Concord Avenue Blues 45
Fool's Gold 47
Race Point 48
apoliticalpoem 49
Partial Rose 50

v

Deserted Beach 51
*The Mind in the Act of Finding
   What Will Suffice* 53
For R 54
Embrace 55
cleave 57
Counterpoint 58
Thorn Apple 59
Remembering Daisies 60
Accoucheuse 61
Rooting 62
Forecast 63
Company 64
Coda: For, as to Change, 65

Sieve 66

TWO ROOMS

SEDIMENTARY BLUES

after Lisel Mueller's "After Whistler"

There are children who should have been stones.
Instead they are put to suck at the cool dugs of water and wind,
Where they are broken down into sediments again—
Silts and clays and loams—
And carefully recast in human form.

Something goes wrong with the heart.
When the other children enter
The long summer grasses in pairs,
From a distance they watch them go,
But soon return to their own solitary
Pleasures—a passion for knowledge or things,
For doing some one thing well.

They are the natural scholars
Teachers love, that parents love
To brag about, although they don't pretend
To understand what God has lodged with them,
Mysterious mute creatures, all memory and cold fire.

While young, the stone-children are able to bear their flesh
With a measure of equanimity and ease,
For then they still believe in its perfecting—
Some intense heat or pressure brought to bear
That will change the body's shale into a slate
Upon which time will write its crystal names.

I

Moving-House Blues

Before being, a place to be in;
Before singing's solace, a wall
Of rock, a stand of pines, a sky
Brim full of unwept tears—
The sheltering structure of song.

For years she had dwelled there:
Grown calm inside its more efficient
Skin, and learned, for the first time
Since fear set in, to breathe
In even measures; she had at last come home.

And the songs she sang—of sea and sky,
Of birds, of trees, and sun—were,
None of them, her own, but riffs
The place had played; she would go forth
Into the world as naked as she came: flayed,

Unhoused, stone-tongued.

Two Rooms

1.
Here where the soul presides
The room is bare but for
A narrow board-hard bed

Which offers no reprieve
From the body's weight, nor yields
An inch to its ripe contours.

Here where the soul presides
No one enters, no one leaves;
There is no door, only

Windows breathing in
The light of an Attic sun.
Here where the soul presides

The body is winnowed at last
Into the absolute. Even
Desire's memory fades;

Nothing troubles your sleep.
All that once you feared to lose
Is long since given away.

2.
In the other room a woman dreams,
Hair tousled, breasts unbound.

A Poem about Brahms Perhaps

Down the long aisle, his Clara on his arm,
No bridal march but German Requiem.

A mannequin with a somewhat narrow heart
Sits at the piano trying the keys
In antiquated locks, frozen for years.

A conscious classicist of abstract forms,
A relic from some prehistoric age—
Miracle he should have a heart at all,

Albeit made of ice. And yet, wonder that
An instrument so small should have such weight—
It pulls his torso low over the keys.

He tries the various keys—the black, the white;
The familiar rhapsodies refuse to fly;
Nothing opens. He tries and tries the keys.

A Portrait

C. P. Cavafy

You keep them well,
In the manner of a young man
Vain about such things, still
Even your hands
Show the wear of time.

Lighting a cigarette,
You move out onto the balcony,
Where you stand—free hand
Loosely held in your trousers' pocket—
For a long time.

As you stare into the darkness,
The city shrugs off
The intervening years
As easily as young men,
Taken by desire,
Shed their clothes in the brothels
Of the Quartier Attirine
Or their fears long enough
To have each other—*delight of flesh*
Through half-opened clothes—
In the seedy public places
Such hungers frequent.

Triolet

Gerard Manley Hopkins

He swore he would not look at stallions
But stallions galloped through his dreams
Their flanks in sun gashed gold, vermillion
He swore he would not look at stallions
But they were everywhere! battalions
Strong: crossing the quad, in choir, at games
He swore he would not look at stallions
But stallions galloped through his dreams

Insomnia

Green-rolling field, ample
Sweet water: you'd enter
The anonymous warm body
Of the fold and hunker there
Dumbly till dawn. You bleat
Your longing, inwardly, but
The gates remain fast against thee.

Skewered on the mind's sharp spit,
You turn and turn. Your eyes
Are glowing coals; in your mouth
The taste of salt and iron. The hunger-
Time has pared illusion down
So that, increasingly, it's hard to hide
What you've become, night after night
Pacing the dark fence line.

Bo Peep Blues

She did not know;
    She did not know;
She asked someone to tell her—
A one she thought might know.

She did not know;
    She did not know;
And none, not one, to spell her.

She climbed into
    The hills by night;
She put the world behind her;

She did not know;
    She did not know,
But cried some God to find her.

Idolatry

To their gods the first fruits,
The first unspotted lamb;

To mine, each day, my hand—
The left, the one I favor—

Launched, as a voice in prayer,
Deep into the well of nothingness:

If I exist, the fingers will close round,
Signed and sealed with love, Reality's

Decrees. Or else I cease to be, addressed
By the mass marketers, *murderers*, I mean.

Too Late, My Mother Tells Me

Those deep lines on your forehead come
From frowning up and reading all the time;
But for them you still look young.
                              Your night-
Time sleep is your life and strength;
You lose your best rest sleeping in the day.
And anyway, if, like you say,
There's no money in it, I wouldn't waste
My time; the book I write will sell.
Best thing, you come on home.

The people I come from have always known
Books and whatnot run some people crazy,
That the mind's a dangerous thing best left alone,
Like blues for some, like sex, like heroin.

Saber-Tooth Blues

Pussycat, but only to you, bright tiger,
I unzip my coat of mail and turn
Sloping underbelly to fire of fang and sun.

Pussycat, but only in the certain grasp,
The gripping force of you,
Your passion's steady blaze . . .

Terror wrangled with desire,
And I proffered you
The bird caged in my throat

That you might teach it sing
The deep, the pure; the keen
And wild bloodnote.

II

From the Land of Shades

Their voices rise and carry across the fields
To where she stands, alone in the almost-dark:
Red Rover, Red Rover, they chant and call her name.

With everything she is she wants to run—
Breaking through the line of arms she'll bring her favorite
Back, and together they will forge another

Chain. Or failing that, they'll take her in,
The body of the fold (O sweet! O warm!)
Moving toward their mothers' calling voices.

Where the others stand she thinks she can see light
(*Red Rover, Red Rover,* they chant and call her name);
The darkness gathers round her, thick and total.

It is her wish to run but something checks her:
The dead do not return from the land of shades.
Red Rover, Red Rover, they chant and call her name.

O Dog of Athens O Belle of Amherst
Traveler in Concord and Faun of the Wood
Link arms with her against that mutton light.

Yeats in Love

Inside, by midmorning, she suffers from
The sulls: she can't sit still, she's underfoot
Or in her mother's hair, or breaking things
She loves—frail emissaries sent to bear
Their love, once precious things grown leaden in
Her hands, dumb hands that have forgotten all
They've known of the gestures of cherishing—
The cheap guitar impossible to tune,
Apple-cheeked dolls bought with books of Green
Stamps saved, the music box her uncle made
That played the song she'd heard her mother sing
So many times it still slowed her breath,
The filaments of song a golden rope
That night after night lowered her to sleep.

Now, nights, she lies wakeful in the silence
Of spring peepers and cricket call, turning
The questions over in her mind: How will
It ever come to her, her life? How find
Her here, in the middle of nowhere where
She's always been—nothing but cows, sky, cow
Manure and corn? And that other wordless
Question, its urgent, constant pressure pressed
Against the length of her so that her mind
And muscles ached. She could keep her bed no more
Than could the adolescent Yeats; she liked
To think of him becoming conscious of
Desire as his body stirred against
The weight of sand he'd buried himself in.

Outside, drowsing in sun, sometimes she dreams
Of bare arms flashing through waves of corn,
Of trees close grown together sheltering her,

Of hands that trail along the smooth, moist walls
Of caves, the body following blind
As bats or moles and just that much at home
In corridors of dark. Or else she lies
Face hidden in the cool declivities
Of hills, a remedy that only feeds
The shame she'd hoped to check. She knows herself
Possessed: Desire belongs to the other one
Who's come to live inside her for a while,
The one that she will nourish, giving all
That she can spare from her own life, much more
Than she can spare—austerity's angel,
Eunuch for the blessed kingdom of her Art.

When Yeats first met Maud Gonne it was as if,
Like Venus rising from the waves, she stepped
Forth from his own body, more beautiful
And larger than he was, more passionate.
He'd given her his life, now she was free
To move toward him across a crowded room,
To touch her hands to his and bring to life
That ancient wholeness first desire cleaves,
And free to turn, redoubling the pain
That time and discipline had somewhat eased.

Phoenix, Daughter of Leda, Amazon,
My wall is loosening; O honey-bees,
Come build in the empty house of the stare.

A Brief Essay on the Economy of Friendship

A friend's hand is open.
—DIOGENES

Meaning: between friends there is nothing to hide:
No little daggers, no salt for wounds, no pride—
The fist closed tight on nothing, pretending to have;

Meaning: not, as most believe, the hand that gives—
The cup of its beneficence is sufficient unto itself—
But the one that bares its emptiness in the grace of being filled;

Meaning: friendship is a commerce carried on by beggars,
Where having nothing each gives all he has
And shamelessly receives all he is given,
The poverty of each a common wealth.

Underwater

Opened their eyes underwater:
Salt-sea burned the scales away
And kept on burning until, realizing
How useless were their eyes,
They gave themselves to dream
And let them close:

Kick of brine against the tender
Lining of mouth and throat, primordial
Hummocks of desire, a hundred
Hands, a herald of rough-tongued
Angels, a thousand candle flames,

Riot of gooseflesh, slow
Golden slide of honey, cooling
Pools of silk. How beautiful
They were!

It is twilight in the room
Or brilliant with fluorescence
Or warm with midday sun;
There are women in the room—
Less than two, more than one.
The women have just met;
They've been talking all their lives
As they are talking now, each to each.

Water rises over their heads;
They do not hold their breaths,
Desiring—supple swimmer
And stony hydrophobe—
This danger, this drowning,
This . . . *stroke by stroke the body*
Remembers . . . home.

This Work of Holding

Leaves no traces, changes nothing
In the world, only alters imperceptibly
The alchemy of souls.
                        Brimming cup,
The body's fire, blessing, bridle,
Bit; the burden and the burden . . .

Major tension, dissonant chord
Between what's given and what's
Withheld—this tender hesitation,
Falling into
              opening out . . .

Rites of Passage

As it is now it has always been

Sailing through the blue/green air
Sailing on the wine/warm sea

Outside as through the passageway
The medium is the same

Inside as through the passageway
The medium is the same

As it is now it has always been

Swimming as you have always swum
Flying as you have flown

As it is now it has always been
As it is now it has *never* been

The red door has disappeared
The blue/green window faded

Wild bird trapped in a human house
Child meshed in inhuman gears

Seeking the hands that would spell release
Fleeing in terror those self-same hands

As it is now it has always been
This frenzy for the door

The Price of the Ticket

We're headed nowhere, as usual—
The shopping mall, the fast-food chain,
The bedroom and the boardroom
Reassuringly the same as those we left.

We're headed nowhere; nevertheless,
We're bound to get there fast,
Hurtling ourselves into the vast
Indifferent reaches of heaven's dome.

An Old One sneezes, blinks an empty eye,
And our wings, no longer wax appendages,
Do not melt away, but flower terribly
Into flame or calcify to stone.

And what falls then is no human thing—
No beautiful boy bruising the ocean's skin
As lovers bruise each other, tenderly;
Nor is it a force of nature,

Though seismographs register the fall.

Burdens

Whatever it was, like summer plumage,
Had long since fallen brightly away.

She hummed inside the knowledge of
Flayed flesh. Everything came close;

She moved away, followed the road
That walking made out past familiar things—

Herself, the outworn childhood names,
The slate and salmon sky she'd known

At evening, bodies donned for warmth.
Whatever it was, a thread unraveled,

As if a baby's fontanel
Refused to close, only softened,

Oozing juices like a rotted pear.
Whatever it was, it didn't matter,

Her long strides lengthened as she climbed
What could have been the face of God—

That smooth, that blank, that cold, that hard.
Her skull became a war of winds;

Her lips cracked, her eyes grew dim.
The only god of that place was wind—

Between mortar and pestle, rock
And wind, being was healed of all

Its weight. The only burdens left
Her are her bones. One by one,

She lays them down at the world's edge
Where waves dance and enchant the stones.

III

The Afterlife

Like not-quite-remembered dream,
That lush, desire-transfigured world
Recedes, leaving us
Not naked, but modestly arrayed
In the ruined theater falling stone from stone.
The seats are empty; the stage is bare;
Unflattering, though not unforgiving is the light.

The words with which we greet each other
—If we greet each other,
As yet unwritten,
We turn the pages over,
Searching silence,
The first tentative syllable of song—

Now that you shall be no god
And I shall not be changed—

Alba

Sing it again, chorus of angels.
Lower your golden ropes that I might climb
Into this day and each day after.

Of music craft for me
A bright windbreaker swift as sail,
A woolen shawl, a sleek new skin.

Lower your ropes and I will climb
Into this sea of leaves and sky;

The oar stands ready, faithful sentinel,
Planted nightly beside my dreaming head.

Improbable Prison's Sweet Mess

Or maybe it was *sweetness* that he meant—
The way the light licked everything, turning
Dross to gold, the curdled milk nacred
Into cream, while potatoes kept on sprouting,
And bread and cheese bloomed bright with mold;
The way the mind pacing its prison finds
A certain sweetness in restraint and calls
Its cage *sweet nest, sweet north, true home* and fouls
The place to mark it as its own, claiming
And defending with daily shit and song:
The soul's silence ratcheted into blues,
The world's fat racket limbed to lullaby.

Poor in All Else . . .

Poor in all else, I feel my thoughts are mine
And will them to no one, but clutch them close
As erstwhile queens clutch jewels, as drunkards wine;

I count them o'er as misers count their coin,
Sullen in having, harried lest they lose
Further estate, and end by having none.

And being none, as men are what they have.

I hear far-off life's choir but cannot join;
Silence, once shawl, has grown a subtle noose;
By holding still I may yet hope survive.

Poor in all else, it's on the heart men dine.

Assimilation Blues

The moon's silver, the sun's plentiful gold,
The splendor of the prince and all his world

Beguiled our eyes until we came to hate
The things of home: the smell of brine, the weight

Of waterlight, the palaces' dank walls
Dripping jewels—corals, ambers, pearls,

And cockle-shells. We let our garden plots,
Much cherished once, run rife with weeds; forgot

The haunting songs our mothers sang, our own
Voices dissonant in our ears; each of us alone

In self-disgust: the scales, the backward tongue,
The fish's tail, the way we swam among

The animals, the lowest ones, soulless
As they were. The old ones grieved for us: solace

We spurned; there was nothing for it but to leave,
And it seemed small sacrifice for us to give

Everything for what we'd get in turn:
Love and a soul.
                Well, live and learn.

Only Human

By the light of the new-minted moon
You dream the fox's dream
Of chickens.

Mornings you bask in the lizard sun
And at the end of summer leave
Your cast-off skin on the cast-
Off river stone.

The owl's slow ghosting cry
Hushes your heart;
You shriek without waking
From your mouse's dream.

Moon at the full,
A lycanthrope, you prowl.

In the end as in the beginning,
The hale abandon the halt
To fang and claw.

Before the Curtain

> The voices have faded with the dusk,
> and night has come like a curtain dropped
> over the brave show of the day, . . .
> the fading certainties of afternoon . . .
> —ELEANOR WILNER, "Transactions in a Field That's Overgrown"

To keep from flagging at their oars
As the last light drains into the sea,
The men are singing as they row:
No more the mighty deeds of war,
But the longed-for pleasures of home—
Hot baths, rich wine, soft beds, and the musk
Of their own women. All day, you cried out
From below. Quiet now, you sit and watch
The waves, your silly task reprieved:
The voices have faded with the dusk.

Apollo's priestess, general's whore,
You keep apart from the other slaves.
Is it pride you feel as you watch him move
Among the men giving orders?
And when you writhe in passion's arms,
All honors, all distinctions stripped
Away, from you, from him, do you
Not love the dumb and dying flesh,
Regret arrival, the death-cry trapped in the throat,
And night come like a curtain dropped?

Like you, we know how the story ends,
And still, like you, we turn the page,
Tracing the plot to its bitter end
In loss and the poverty of dust.
The reading, once so natural, now
Comes hard; we falter, question why,

As we watch you walk that longest mile
From chariot to palace door
Where nothing, nothing can stay those hands.
Over, the brave show of the day.

The hands of the clock say half past four
When we shift in our ergonomic chairs;
An hour ago attention frayed;
Now self-doubt swarms like angry wasps
As ambition mocks what the day has made.
It's just the going of the sun
That wakes the infant of the soul;
Quick now, sugar, before she howls—
Chocolate, bourbon, scotch—against
The fading certainties of afternoon.

The Pack

> Short the way, but pitiless
> The need to walk it.
> —ALKMAN

There is no stream; there is no end in sight.
The lonely mountain path winds on and on.
Breath catches in the lungs like fine-ground glass;
The solemn climber gulps it down like wine.
Still, his head is light, his muscles burn.
The pack he carries drags his body down.

Departure was clear morning, dawn itself.
A human frankness about the look of things.
At least that's what he'd thought, companions round,
Drinking coffee, making ready in first light.
The pack he carried then was like a sail;
The mountains, seas at rest, more merciful.

In another poem perhaps there'd be a stream.
Perhaps a little clearing in a wood:
The climber casts his burdens to the ground
And bathes his feet in the waters of the stream.
He rests a long time there under the leaves,
And going on again, he travels light.

In another poem perhaps, but in this one
There is no stream; the path winds on and on.
And the climber doesn't know just why he climbs
Or why he cannot take the path back down.
He doesn't know what happened to those friends
Or the human frankness in the look of things.

He knows the teeth of winds, the rocks below,
The solid purchase, hard-won by his feet.

He knows at some point each one climbs alone
And that there must be others up ahead.
He knows the pack is added to each mile.
He knows no prayer to brake or break a fall.

A Song of Brothers
A Duet

There is no end to sorrow.
—VAN GOGH

Heavy he is and swift
The current, sweeping us
Farther out to sea;
Terrible, mysterious,
This hold he has on me.
Heavy he is and slow
The going, one stroke forward,
Waves drive us back. Sorrow
Sucks us down and down,
My muscles fail, go slack.
I have a child now of my own;
To carry on my back.

Heavy it is to bear
Such cargo, three souls held
Inside one breast: Vincent
That sleeps in the cold churchyard,
The other that might as well.
Heavy it is and far
The harbor; winds buffet
From every side; no star
Lights us home. I'll cut
The towrope soon, not long,
And then, Theo, you'll see, it was
My weakness made you strong.

Brother, here, I give you freedom,
Spend it on your son and wife;
Brother, don't let go I'm drowning,
Your art gave my life life.

Stove

Blessed is he who blithely
Weaves his day straight through
Without a tear.
—ALKMAN

Sometimes the mind, hemmed in
At every side, throws itself,
Repeatedly and hard,
Against the barrier
Of skull, desperate to feel
The easy downhill rush
Of rivers, not
The hectic spiraling
Of thought inside
An unsolvable maze.

A gale force wind batters
Windows and door—
Both temples and forehead—
Until the whole bloom quakes,
And the stalk on which it's held,
In order to sustain
The aching weight,
Clenches all its fibers.

Once upon a time
The mind of man did make
Its dwelling-place far
From such precipitate heights:
The soles of unshod feet,
The murky swamp of sex,
The body's central stove,

The solar plexus, or
The heart that sings inside
Its bone cathedral.

Perched high above the body,
The mind cannot know
Itself, nor live quite in
The living shelter Earth
Provides, instead must make
Of Earth an Anti-Earth:
From pure streams, a poison,
From singing trees, a dumbness;
One all-consuming numbness
From pleasure and from pain.

Like the madwoman
Imprisoned in the attic,
The mind paces, biding
Its sweet time. Then
It springs, breeding
Explosions, roofs blown off.

Is Backing Away. Is Gone

By the sweet neck-scruff it had you:
Brimstone breath and then the fang
Going in, lifted up and carried.

Death then this, you thought, already dead,
Dread turning over into glee,
Good the primal maw, annihilation.

The beast bounds off, scenting
Other prey. Dropped, you lay
There sweating in the leaves.

A far-off death-scream makes
A passage in your heart.
As light lightens, you watch

Them as they come, as if
To the edge of a stream to drink,
The lion and the lamb,

All bloodlust done, peaceably
To sleep in the heart's bright lair.

The Wheel

1. *Raw winter wind*

Raw winter wind
  Asking, asking
Parched as Sahara,
   Lonely as the sun.

Raw winter wind
  Asking, asking
Recalcitrant mountains,
   Merciless moon.

2. What She Prayed For:

An angel, rain, a kangaroo

3. Rising Late

This morning, sun—
The weight of it and warm—
Upon my back as I
Lay late abed.

I can't remember when
And wish it would—
Some human hand
To touch me as the sun does.

4. Flute, Lamp, Chalice, Urn

Turned on desire's wheel,
Clay vessels take the shape of loss;
  Crack, endure, splinter,
    Shine in being's brutal kiln.

IV

As If I Had Invented It

I sent out hope to usher in the spring;
I stitched the threads of gold in summer's gown;
It was my joy that taught the birds to sing;
My sole largess that rounded nature's horn.
Now my sullen thoughts turn grasses brown;
My restlessness sets winds to quarreling;
My worry pinches faces in the town—
Crows cry warnings, woodsmen's axes ring.
Because I turn from light, the darkness gathers.
Without the warmth I give the world grows cold.
Because I do not care, nothing matters—
Innocence betrayed, betrays the world.
    However well I love, ere long I lose,
        So I've sworn me out a patent on the blues.

From the Monk's Courtship

1. Three Kisses

     i.
Unworthy of the dust
Unworthy to look up
Unworthy to beseech
Thy hand, thy grace

Belly over ground
Like the subtle worm I am

I press unworthy lips
Against thy feet

     ii.
Thy hand is milk and honey
Thy hand is freckled and brown
Thy hand is soft as lambs' wool
Thy hand is harder than iron

Thy hand is cool and fragrant
Thy hand is warmer than sun
Thy hand is dry as deserts
My lips are two cracked stones

My lips are anxious pilgrims
Maddened by thirst, mirage, and sun
Thy hand
    fountain, gourdvine, parchment

The way is written on

iii.
You bend and lift
Until we stand

Lip to lip
Breast to breast

True god to true god
Word to flesh

One being in embrace
Inseparable

2. An Apology

Suggestive bed,
two chaste chairs:
between them,
         nothing,
no common ground
where two might sit
—as if under the high
spice-trees of summer—
shoulder to shoulder, hip
to hip, not speaking so much
as spoken by
         the supple tongues
of leaves and grasses,
the redolent syllable
of summer itself:

a stillness, a being still,
before the time of lying,
that heavy ripeness
that drags all bodies down.

3. On Rapture

It begins as revelation:
Scored with new light, a world
Newer than morning, fresher than spring—
An astonishment of singing.

It begins in radiance:
The holocaust of light you enter gladly,
Eager to be consumed by The Shining One,
The Ravenous, The Radically Alive.

A counterfeit grace, this swift unburdening,
But who could not be moved
By the useless severed head
So prettily arranged upon a silver plate?

Only Where There Is Floating

Drifting in the widening wake
Of your own disappearing trail

Yourself diaphanous, abstract
The river all the world

So suddenly the landscape shifts
Softened by the water's suit

The bank soughs beneath your feet
But this is not for poetry

If it be a trail
Cheek's contour, jut of chin

Swan's down or bristle
Hands given over

A woman's face

Lying

awake at 4 a.m.
whatever the space beside you holds
you are   yourself   alone

and whatever there is of truth
turning in crevices light can't touch
it must be that which wakes you

      *

in a quiet room a woman works
arranging words, a world
where she might live

it changes little day to day
but the mind is changed
as light changes, as the leaves turn

and whatever holds that space inside her
it is so much harder, vaster, colder
than this near mortal, however breathing, however loved.

Concord Avenue Blues

1. Wake

I hate your sleep,
oblivion you marry
too eagerly, too often,

the way the air hangs thick with it,
my own limbs grown heavy.

I hate your sleep,
our wasted days, your
epic snoring.

I hate your sleep.
Hate the magic pills
that row you out
into deep water.

I love it when you stretch yourself and rise.

2. At Home

I move through rooms
as if by stealth
removing traces
of where I've been;

You are a whirlwind passing.

You loose demons
of distraction in a house
of contemplation;

where silence waited
arrival of right words,
day and night
ciphers din and hiss.

At home, you settle in;
I wander streets in rain.

3. Blues

Each night that I'm away
sleep in my blue night shirt.
I will sleep in nothing—
if I sleep at all—
except the scent of you.

*Brilliant, elusive
as a Bird of Paradise,
manna from heaven,
honey on the tongue—
always knew you'd leave.*

Fool's Gold

As once a child you relished childish things,
In reverie you surf the Net for toys—
If only sex were somehow interesting.

It almost turns you on remembering
The mysteries of girls, the thrum of boys
When as a child you played at childish things,

But that, that wasn't real: imagining
Some pure, ethereal sweet that wouldn't cloy.
If only sex were somehow interesting.

Are we there yet? What can we do? It's boring.
Sure bullion in the bank becomes alloy
As when a child you tired of childish things.

Change positions, partners, sexes; fling
Inhibitions, morals to the wind. Joy.
If only sex were somehow interesting.

Methodically you play, no heart for playing—
Desire's game an unremitting toil
As when a child you aped grim grown-up things
And dreamed that sex was so, so interesting.

Race Point

"Are you able to see the moon and stars?"
"I can see the moon."

What eludes purpose is found by accident:
As the shape of a line or a road taken at evening
That leads past the empty booth of the parking attendant
To this morning's thwarted goal:
A sandy beach fronting the Atlantic.

Earlier all roads had led to Herring Cove—
Its sheltered waters, its beach more rock than sand
(Impossible to walk on!)—or so it seemed.

Now the sand is fine beneath your feet;
The evening cool, the beach deserted—
A smattering of bonfires people the night
And, intermittently, the glaring headlights of the beach patrol,
But for all intents and purposes you are alone . . .

Later, wanting to see what she sees,
I turn my eyes to the night sky
And for the first time see the stars.

apoliticalpoem

you can always write your confessional

x marks the spot, center of the world
somebody done somebody, apple of my eye

wrong poem

can always say the light this morning
the light this morning, her breast, wild plum
in lamplight, moonlight, birdsong

can always say the light this morning
unless no sun; her breast, wild plum
unless no breast where lush full flesh had been

life won't wait around forever
but it will wait awhile

forsake the bed where one you love is sleeping
taking instead to wife the dire headlines, late-
breaking updates on the hour and half hour
endless speculation on uncorroborated, nonspecific threats

weep wail rage against injustice
grieve for the poor who are always with us
let righteous indignation kindle your heart
focus; will this fire to purify the world

a hand on your shoulder breaks the spell
robe fallen open, warm sleep smell
a flawed world perfect, perfect as it is
though not by us perfectible

Partial Rose

March 16, 2003

We've forced the bud
bruised the petals
no rose shall ever listen here
its choir of mouths cry open
to bless us or accuse
we chose another life
the palest flowers
ash, snow, the un
cut hair of graves

V

Deserted Beach

after William Merritt Chase

waves fall at earth's
knees beseeching
again again
like well-whipped egg
whites froth glistens

gulls wheel dive their
grating music
harrows livens
misted morning
air overwhelms
silence roiling
chest deep in this
borrowed room where
I wake alone

the grate is cold
curtains riffle
aimless pages
in a battered
notebook cork mis-
laid colors flat

I long to sweep
up errant sand
spill it down time's
narrow gullet
the floor bare clean
again as smooth
as well-kissed stones
blank as the day's
blue unfolding
beloved face
turning away

The Mind in the Act of Finding What Will Suffice

Seizes summer,
                an evening in late summer
Where cicadas choired
                      and the company fell away
As darkness settled
                round us like a shawl
And our voices found
                another register
Below the pitch
              and roll of social chatter. . . .
And life in that new place seemed possible
Because it held within it something old,
Companionable—cat's purr, horse's nicker—
The words we speak to hold each other close
As darkness swallows the world and pares
Us back to the merest husk of creature being.

I'm old enough to know it wasn't love,
Wasn't much of anything at all,
Yet just before sleep or waking up
Or sitting at my desk dreaming lines,
I find myself inexorably drawn
As if below this life, an underlife—
Fierce, heedless, hidden, shy of sun—
Suddenly stretched its sinuous length and ran
Along the neural pathways breathing flame.

For R

What makes one woman
a cool green hill
you long to burrow into;
another hard transparent
glass you sail straight through
with only minor consequences?

Surely I have lived a life of joy with you . . .
but when I think of you now
it is of hurt places,
gentle articulate hands.

Embrace

Turning in upon myself to sleep
Again again I walk into the arms
Of a woman whose presence moved me:
In unaccustomed gesture I reach up,
And she, cupped hand cradling the base of my skull,
Brings my head to rest against her shoulder.

I rest against her shoulder
Years later wanting sleep,
Wanting the racket in my skull—
Vague rumblings, reasoned thought, alarms—
To hush, be quiet, dry up,
For consciousness, dear God, at last to leave me.

Her presence hurt me—
My name, my back, my shoulder:
Each caress a waking up
In springtime after hard winter sleep.
I walk into her arms;
We sway a little, murmur, her warm hand cups my skull.

Pain's source and salve compounded in my skull,
Sometimes I fear some sickness deep in me.
Again again I fold into her arms
Or rest my head on some imagined shoulder;
Still, no rest, no sleep;
Need, insatiable virus, keeps me up

Until heedless, precipitate I look her up,
Expose the meager flame in the skull's
Cave. The light flares, goes out. *Hush now, sleep.*
No earthly use. She has no use for me.

Still, as we sat together in a crowded room, she traced circle after circle around my
    shoulder
Blade; she covered my hand, slipped me a colored stone; shook loose her hair for me;
    sought me out; remarked my beauty; read me Stevens and her own elusive poems;
    gathered me in her arms.

And could you choose never to have known those arms . . . ?
The fever would still rise, driving the mercury up,
Its chills and sweats shaking your sturdy shoulders,
Eroding discipline—music, Latin, logic—I-beams to support a caving skull.
Sometimes I fear some sickness deep in me.
Turning in upon itself to sleep,

It howls like a babe-in-arms possessed and suckles at the marrows of my skull.
I tuck it up and hold it close to me;
The weight of it pulls my shoulders down, drags me off toward some final sleep.

cleave

she wants to graze you in her going
   not wake but stir
      not rouse but worry
         ever slightly the surface of dream

clipped call-note, half-swallowed
   cheep, briefest brush of breath
      against your cheek, not shadow
         but a shadow of the shadow of wings

somewhere a woman is dying
   (or thinks she is) she imagines
      touch (yours) might stay her
         is it willfully you misunderstand?

we fail each other in the smallest things.

Counterpoint

It was always dark then
silence deepened   notes
rushed the room like water
nights listening reading
the life of Brahms   as if
it were her own palm
scored with Braille and all
she might become through rage
of will was mirrored there
a dark page punched with holes.

Thorn Apple

rose rosebud conrose
my father's names for me
rose of sharon compass rose
rilke's great rose windows
rosewater clean
sharpsweet as rain
rosie my grandma
my ma'amaw's name
crowrose my new christening
a name as dark as plush as wings
rosewing grosbeak
knife edge flame tongue
ruddy bloodblack molasses
partial rose my requiem
rose to the occasion
rose bruise of persuasion
blue elusive rose of grace
grim elation cabbage rose
feels good enough to ride
soft rose of a horse's mouth
unfathomable roseate eyes
darkroom roses
rose of silence
violent rose
a nose for roses
a rose for noses
a nosegay one might say
rosebud comet dying flame

Remembering Daisies

After the blameless flower
is but a picked-clean stalk,
you regret the glut of petals
squandered, one by one—
quarters recklessly flung
in a children's wishing well—:
loves me, loves me not?

As if that were the question,
the answer brilliantly
arrayed around the day's
plush eye. As if it weren't
the mind that cleaves the splendid
one-in-many into two—
always and only two.

As if it weren't the fear-
torn heart that begs the jaded
question: *loves me, loves me
not,* not *do I love?*
You might have braided, stalk
by stalk, a daisy chain,
to crown the one you loved,

a cliff walk to the farther side of fear

Accoucheuse

For Ella Magruder

We have slept so long
waiting to give birth
wanting to be born
one huge with expectancy
the other shadow thin
unreal almost nonexistent

Who can say what stirs us
begins the long hard laboring
but you are there a voice
strict admonishment sermon lullaby
that answers every effort
steadies our wavering coaches our breath

Focused fierce miraculous you only have to say *massage*
to release scrunched shoulders lengthen crumpled neck
and more than any temperature or texture
one might name your hands are sure
centering the cattywampus head
tilting the shoulders just so to realign the spine

making ready making room hauling something new into this life

Rooting

October baby stalling into
far reaches of November,
you didn't want to be born,
but now since your life ended
brilliant September afternoon
but stopped short of a sudden
shy of death and autumn banked
its blazes into ashen winter
dormant spring you root
in still cold ground this time
a scrappy premie suckling
piglet first fierce volunteer.

Forecast

On the bank of the Charles
inhaling the weather
which includes the sun
and the sun on water
and the long week of rain
just past
      she is thinking
of two women, recently met,
of startling plumage
and names like Mabel or Jane

the ache of possibility
nothing yet exhausted
the endlessness of need

to come into the circle
of her and her attention
how or when she cannot fathom
but knows that it must be.

Company

Not the kind whose coming
unleashes flurries
of furious cleaning

nor the kind that blithely
owns the mill, the mine,
the store, that trades in souls

but the easy kind of sisters, one
settled on the top-down toilet,
the other ensconced in the tub,
taking turns, keeping each other
company while taking a bath

or the man who stops by the fence
to pass the time of day
with a woman wrist deep
in the dirt of her garden

they have a laugh together
then in the wake of a pause
he asks her when she thinks
she'll be wanting
company

and though, gently,
graciously, she hands
him back his offer
and feels a twinge of sorrow
as he moves away crestfallen,
there is that sweetness still.

Coda
For, as to Change,

No, *we would not be God's locusts*
Living all those seasons in the dark;
But say the soul's a great mosaic
Shattered in the atmosphere at birth,
And life the search, the slow and tedious,
Never-ending work of gathering
—*There was a child went forth everyday,*
And the first object he look'd upon,
    that object he became—
Something beautiful and various
Beyond the niggling smallnesses of self:
The way I shall be less without the circle
    of her regard;
As, Blessèd, I should be, bereft of yours.

SIEVE

Light
   in autumn
that stand
   of trees
in leaf
   blossom
bare, flare
   Of bone
that woman's
   wing, beneath
brief moment
   fingers splayed
your out-
   stretched palm

fraying heart
   an errant
strand, hairbrush
   mislaid
a river
   braided
gray brown gold

you catch
   It up
as if to drink

   quick
silver
   spills
from your hand

www.ingramcontent.com/pod-product-compliance
Lightning Source LLC
Chambersburg PA
CBHW022110160426
43198CB00008B/417